I Saw You in the
BATHTUB
AND OTHER FOLK RHYMES

An I Can Read Book®

I Saw You in the
BATHTUB

AND OTHER FOLK RHYMES

Collected by Alvin Schwartz

Pictures by Syd Hoff

Harper & Row, Publishers

For Bill Morris

Foreword

This book is filled with rhymes.

They are silly and funny

and scary.

Nobody knows who made them up.

But some of the poets were children.

Their rhymes were passed

from person to person.

And now they have reached you.

Maybe some day

you will write a rhyme

like one of these.

I saw you in the street,

I saw you in a tree,

I saw you in the bathtub—

Whoops! Pardon me!

I know a boy,

His name is Bill,

Never took a bath

And never will.

Ach, poo! Dirty Bill.

One,

Two,

Three,

Four,

Five,

Six,

Seven,

All good children go to heaven.

When they get there they repeat,

"Way up here you wash your feet!"

My father is a butcher,

My mother cooks the meat,

I'm a little hot dog

That runs down the street.

I had a little dog,

His name was Spot,

Whenever we cooked,

He licked the pot.

Me, myself and I

Sneaked into the kitchen

And ate a pie.

Then my mother she came in

And chased me out

With a rolling pin.

Mary, Mary, strong and able,

Keep your elbows off the table.

This is not a horse's stable.

16

I scream,

You scream,

We all scream

For ice cream!

Now I lay me down to sleep,

A bag of peanuts at my feet.

If I die before I wake,

I will have died of a bellyache.

18

Old man Moses, sick in bed,

Called the doctor,

And the doctor said,

"Old man, old man, you're not sick,

All you need is a licorice stick."

19

Oh, I stuck my head

In a little skunk's hole,

And the little skunk said,

"Well, bless my soul.

Take it out!

Take it out!

Take it out!

Remove it!"

20

When I did not take it out,

The little skunk said,

"You had better take it out,

Or you'll wish you were dead.

Take it out!

Take it out!

Take it out!

Remove it!"

I removed it....

Ssssssssssssssssssssssssssss.

TOO LATE!

I am a little chestnut brown

Lying on the cold, cold ground.

Somebody came and stepped on me,

Now I am as cracked as I can be.

I am a nut *click, click,*

I am a nut *click, click,*

A nut,

A nut,

A nut *click, click.*

(To make a clicking sound,

just snap your fingers.)

Ooey Gooey was a worm.

Ooey Gooey loved to squirm.

Squirmed up on the railroad track,

Squirmed around on his back.

Along came a train

Clickety-clack.

OOEY GOOEY!

Three little chickadees

Looking at you,

One flew away

And then there were two.

Two little chickadees

Sitting in the sun,

One flew away

And then there was one.

One little chickadee

Sitting all alone,

She flew away

And then there were none.

27

Count the birds in a tree.

They will tell you

What is to be.

One for sadness,

Two for joy,

Three for a girl,

Four for a boy,

Five for silver,

Six for gold,

Seven for a secret

That has never been told.

Polly had a dolly

Who was sick, sick, sick.

She called the doctor

Quick, quick, quick.

The doctor came with his bag and his hat,

Rapped on the door

With a rat-a-tat-tat.

Looked at the dolly,

Shook his head,

Said, "Polly, put her straight to bed!"

Rain on the green grass,

Rain on the tree,

Rain on the housetops,

But not on me.

Ladybug, ladybug, fly away home,

Your house is on fire

And your children have flown—

All but one

And her name is Joan,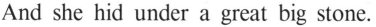

And she hid under a great big stone.

Teacher, teacher made a mistake—

She sat down in a chocolate cake!

34

"Tattletale, ginger ale,

Stick your head in a garbage pail!"

"Kindergarten baby,

Stick *your* head in gravy!"

"Call me this, call me that,

Call yourself a dirty rat!"

Someone is under the bed!

Whoever can it be?

I am getting very nervous.

"Sally, come in with me."

Sally crawled under the bed.

Whoever did she see?

"There is someone here," she said.

"But I think it is me!"

There was a boy

Who would not go to bed,

His eyes got so tired,

They fell from his head.

Down in the desert

Where the purple grass dies,

There sat a witch

With yellow-green eyes.

It was the night of Halloween

When all the witches could be seen.

Some were black, some were green,

Some were like a turkey bean.

41

"Crybaby, crybaby,

Wipe your little eye,

Go and tell your mommy

To give you a piece of pie."

"Baby, baby, suck your toe

All the way to Mexico.

When you get there, cut your hair,

And don't forget your underwear."

Here is a beehive.

Where are the bees?

Hiding away where nobody sees.

They are coming out now.

One,

Two,

Three,

Four,

Five!

I am bringing home a bumblebee.

Won't my mother be pleased with me!

I am bringing home—

Ouch! It stung me!

I am squashing up a bumblebee.

Won't my mother be pleased with me!

I am squashing up—

Ick!

I am eating up a bumblebee.

Won't my mother be pleased with me!

I am eating up—

Ooooh! My stomach!

Round as a cookie,

Busy as a bee,

What on earth

Can it be?

(Turn the page

for the answer.)

A watch!

When I was a little boy,

I washed my mother's dishes.

I put my finger in my ear

And pulled out little fishes.

My mother called me a good boy,

She told me to do it again.

I put my finger in my ear

And pulled out a big fat hen.

"Green eye, pickle pie,

Run around and tell a lie!"

"Don't be mean, jellybean."

53

Bubble gum, bubble gum,

Chew and blow.

Bubble gum, bubble gum,

Scrape your toe.

Bubble gum, bubble gum,

Tastes so sweet—

Get that bubble gum

Off your feet.

A, B, C, D,

E, F, G,

H, I, J, K,

L, M, N, O, P,

Q, R, S, T,

U

are

It!

One, two, three,

Look out for me!

I'm going to find you

Wherever you be!

Silence in the court

While the judge blows his nose

And stands on his head

And tickles his toes.

When you come to the end of a lollypop,

And sit alone with the stick,

Just think of all the other ones

That someday you will lick.

Sally go round the sun,

Sally go round the moon,

Sally go round the chimney top

On a Saturday afternoon.

KA-BOOM!

WHERE THE RHYMES COME FROM

These rhymes are from California, Indiana, Kansas, Maine, Maryland, Massachusetts, Michigan, New Jersey, Ohio, Pennsylvania, and Texas, and also Canada and England. But they could have come from many other places.

The second verse of "Someone Is Under the Bed!" was written by me. Have fun!

ABOUT THE AUTHOR

Alvin Schwartz has compiled many books for young readers on folklore and folk humor, including five other Harper I CAN READ titles: *Ten Copycats in a Boat and Other Riddles*; *Busy Buzzing Bumblebees and Other Tongue Twisters*; *There Is a Carrot in My Ear and Other Noodle Tales*; *All of Our Noses Are Here and Other Noodle Tales*; and the best-selling *In a Dark, Dark Room and Other Scary Stories.*

Mr. Schwartz and his wife live in Princeton, New Jersey.

ABOUT THE ILLUSTRATOR

Syd Hoff has written as well as illustrated numerous books for children, among them the beloved classic I CAN READ Books *Danny and the Dinosaur*; *Who Will Be My Friends?*; *Sammy the Seal*; and *Oliver.* He is also well known for his Early I CAN READ Books, including *The Horse in Harry's Room*; *Mrs. Brice's Mice*; and *Barney's Horse.*

A native of New York City, Mr. Hoff now lives in Miami Beach.

64